The Adarna is a unique and wonderful bird in Philippine folklore. It can change the color of its feathers into more radiant and enchanting shades. Its song is so entrancingly sweet it can induce one to sleep. And once its droppings fall on someone, he will surely turn into stone. But the same song can cure the most serious illness one can think of.

Our story here tells of how Don Juan, one of the Berbanian princes, was able to catch the enchanted bird whose song would cure his ailing father. Recommended for children three to ten years old.

ADARNA BOOKS

Copyright © 1983 Children's Communication Center, Victoria Añonuevo and Nori Millare. All rights reserved, including the use and reproduction in any form or manner, except with written permission from the copyright owners.

First printing of the first edition
Made and printed in the Philippines
Published by the Children's Communication Center
in cooperation with the Cultural Center of the Philippines

Sonrisa · 63
Published by MARUZEN Mates Co. Ltd. in Japan

the MAGICAL SONG of the ADARNA

Retold by Victoria Anonuevo
Illustrated by Nori Millare

ADARNA BOOKS

Children's Communication Center
P.O. Box 10011 Quezon City, Philippines

A long, long time ago,
a king named Fernando
ruled the kingdom of Berbania.
The king ruled well and wisely
that for years, the kingdom
was very peaceful and prosperous.

The king had three sons
all worthy as heirs to the royal throne.
The eldest, Don Pedro, was brave and strong.
Don Diego, the second, was an excellent hunter.
Don Juan, the youngest, was kind and helpful.
Among the three, it was Don Juan
who was loved by all.

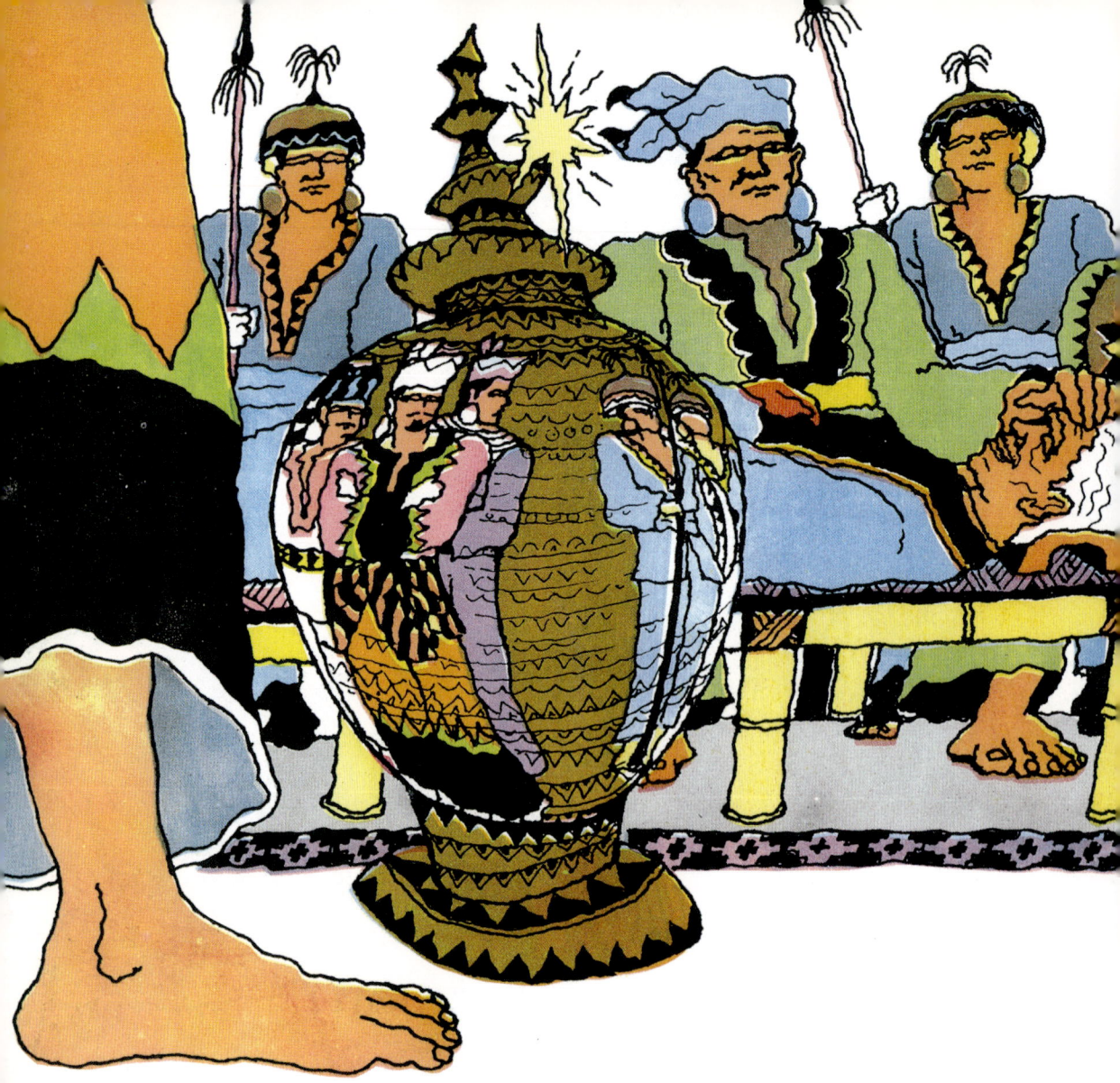

One day, King Fernando suddenly fell ill.
And what a strange and serious illness!
Not even the best doctors in the kingdom
could make the king well.
The three princes watched helplessly
as the doctors showed hopelessness
over the condition of the king.
Everyone in the kingdom wept and prayed.

Then a wise-looking old man
came to the palace to see the ailing king.
"Well," said Don Pedro, "can you get him well?"
"There's only one thing that can cure His Majesty,"
the old man said.
"Then out with it!" demanded Don Diego.
"We will do everything to save our father,"
Don Juan said worriedly.

"The song of the adarna!" replied the old man,
"Its magical song will make the king well."
"What is an adarna?" asked Don Pedro.
"Adarna is a bird of wonder," said the old man.
"Where can we buy such a bird?" asked Don Pedro.
"My dear Highness," explained the old man,
"no amount of money can buy the adarna.
It is an enchanted and elusive bird,
one must persevere to catch it."
"Where can we find it?" asked Don Diego.
"The adarna lives in the tree of Piedras Platas
on the high peaks of Mount Tabor."
"Then I will leave at once to look for it,"
declared Don Pedro.
"Be prepared, Your Highness," warned the old man,
"for the journey will be long and difficult."
"My courage has not yet failed me," said Don Pedro.

And so Don Pedro set for his journey.
He crossed many rivers and forests
but he could not find Mount Tabor.
He asked everyone he met about the mountain
but no one knew what or where it was.
Suddenly, a wretched old man appeared on the way.
The old man's long white hair had become grey
because of the sun, wind and dust.
His skin was heavily wrinkled, warted and freckled,
with dirty rashes and lesions.
He wore a tattered sackcloth that was also dirty.
"Young man, please help me,"
the old man begged Don Pedro.
"I am very hungry and thirsty,
a little food and water are all I need."

"Huh, do not come near me, old man,"
exclaimed Don Pedro, "I am a prince
and it is not proper for a dirty beggar
like you to come near me."
"Please young man, only a little food
and water, please help me. . ."
"I need every food and water
to last for my whole journey.
And even if have more,
I would not dare give them to you.
So go away, go away!"

The old man was about to turn away
when Don Pedro said, "Wait, old man!
Do you know where Mount Tabor is?"
The old man pointed to the tall blue mountain
that was lying in the east.
"That is Mount Tabor," the old man said.
"Now may I have a few drops of water?"
"As I told you old man," replied Don Pedro,
"the water here is just enough for me."
Then he quickly headed for Mount Tabor.

It was already evening when Don Pedro
reached the top of Mount Tabor.
And there it was: the amazing tree!
Its leaves were silk with gold linings,
while its silvery trunk and branches
were sequined with sparkling diamonds and sapphires.
"This must be the tree of Piedras Platas,"
Don Pedro gasped as he marvelled at the tree.
Tired but excited, he sat beside a white stone
and waited for the arrival of the enchanted bird.

Moments later, Don Pedro heard
a fluttering of wings on top of the Piedras Platas.
And as he looked up, he saw the most beautiful bird
he had ever seen in his whole life.
"The adarna bird! The adarna bird!"
The adarna was like a queen in full regalia.
It had a foam-like crown with diamond studs.
Its feathers were strong, thick and shiny;
while its long fern-like tail hung
like an embroidered wedding train of a royal bride.

Then, the adarna began to sing.
It was the sweetest and most melodious song
that Don Pedro ever heard.
Seven times did its feathers change colors —
ruby red, sunset orange, peach yellow,
emerald green, satin blue, velvet violet
and deep indigo — and while this was going on,
Don Pedro slowly dropped off to sleep.
No one could keep him from sleeping
once he heard the song of the enchanted bird!

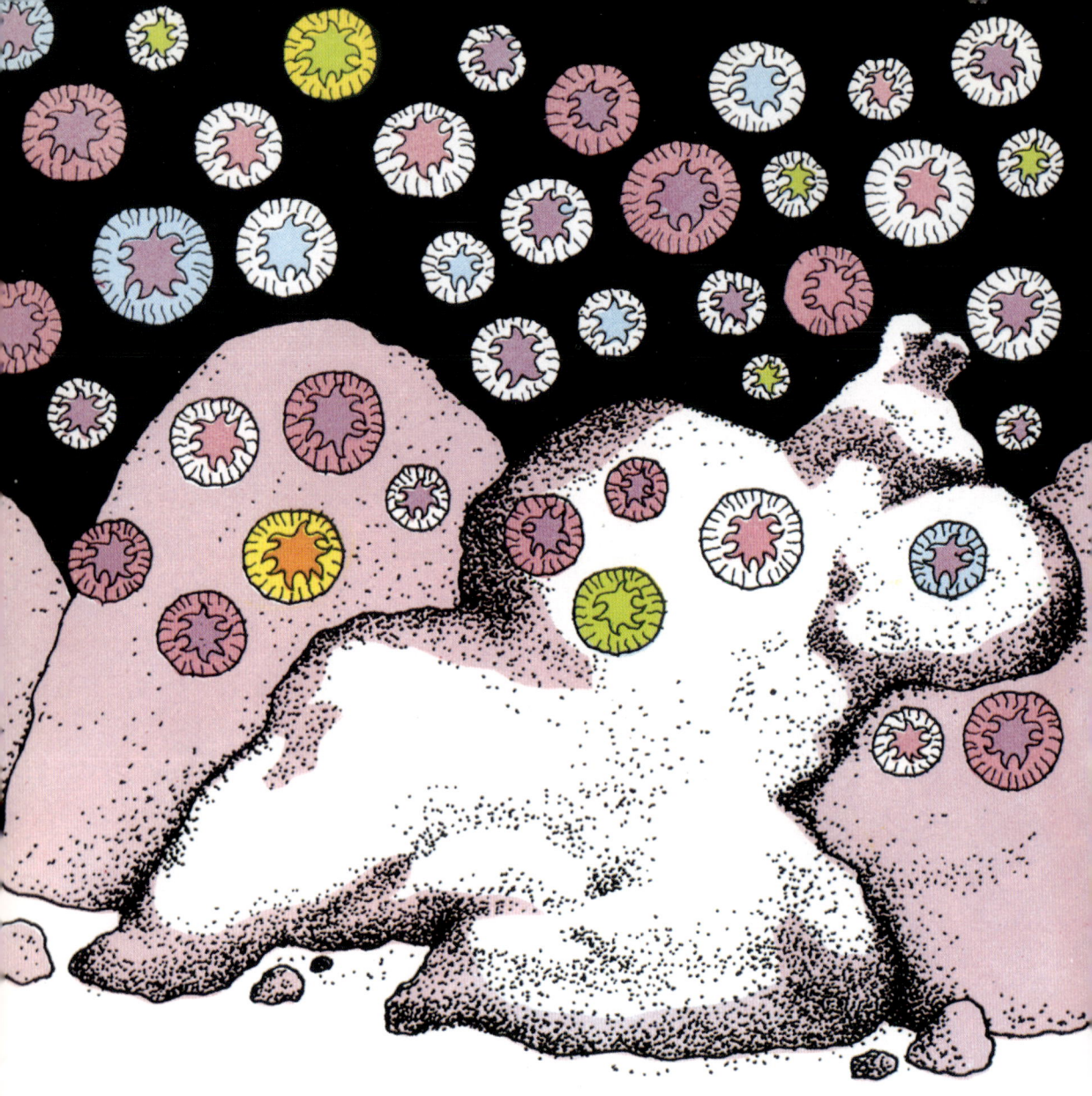

As soon as it finished its last song,
the adarna excreted and proceeded to sleep.
But alas! the bird's droppings fell
on the sleeping Don Pedro.
And Don Pedro turned into a huge white stone!

When Don Diego followed,
he had the same fate that Don Pedro had.
He suffered many difficulties along the way.
He met the wretched old man
and ignored the old man's pleadings.
And when he found the adarna in Piedras Platas,
he too fell asleep while wondering at the sight
and listening to the songs of the enchanted bird.
Don Diego also turned into a stone!

Back in the palace, Don Juan was restless.
"My father is getting weaker and weaker.
And there is no word about my brothers.
I must go and find them myself," he thought.

Like his brothers, Don Juan met
the wretched old man who pleaded,
"Water, please, water..."
The young prince led the old man
to a shade under a tree.
There, he let the old man drink from his flask.
He also laid some bread for the old man to eat.
"But you too have to eat," said the old man.
"Don't worry," Don Juan said calmly,
"I am young and strong. You need the food
and water more than I do."

Suddenly, the old man's appearance changed.
Gone were the dirty clothes and sores
   that had so disgusted Don Pedro and Don Diego.
"You are the old man who told us
   to look for the adarna bird!" Juan exclaimed.
"Yes, Your Highness," the old man explained,
"I stood on this path to test you and your brothers.
   Because you have the kindest heart of all,
   I will help you catch the adarna bird."

"Take these," said the old man,
  showing Don Juan a dagger, a lemon fruit
  and a vial of blessed water.
"When the adarna starts to sing,"
  the old man continued,
"cut your arms slightly with the dagger
  then rub the lemon juice on the wounds.
  It will keep you awake."
"What will I do with the holy water?" asked Don Juan.
"Sprinkle it to the big white stones
  under the tree of Piedras Platas."
"Stones?" asked Don Juan.
"The stones were formerly humans
  until the droppings of the adarna
  fell on them," explained the old man.

At last, Don Juan reached Mount Tabor.
Like his brothers, Don Juan marvelled
at the majestic sight of the place.
A few moments later, the adarna flew in.
"Yes," Don Juan thought, "yes,
the adarna is the most beautiful bird!"
The bird sat on one of the big branches.
Don Juan breathlessly hid behind a big stone.

Again, the adarna began to sing.
As it sang, its glossy plummage
started to change colors seven times.
The sweetness of the song
made Don Juan's eyelids grow heavy.
But he remembered the words of the old man!
He slightly cut his arms and squeezed lemon juice
on the wound. It sharpened the pain!
And just as the old man said,
the unbearable pain kept him wide awake!

Then, the adarna closed its eyes.
Don Juan slowly set to catch it.
Then he remembered the words of the old man,
"The adarna excretes before its sleeps."
And just as the bird did its sleeping ritual,
Don Juan was able to stay away and avoid
the bird's droppings that turned humans into stones.
Then he climbed up the tree
and succeeded in catching the enchanted bird.

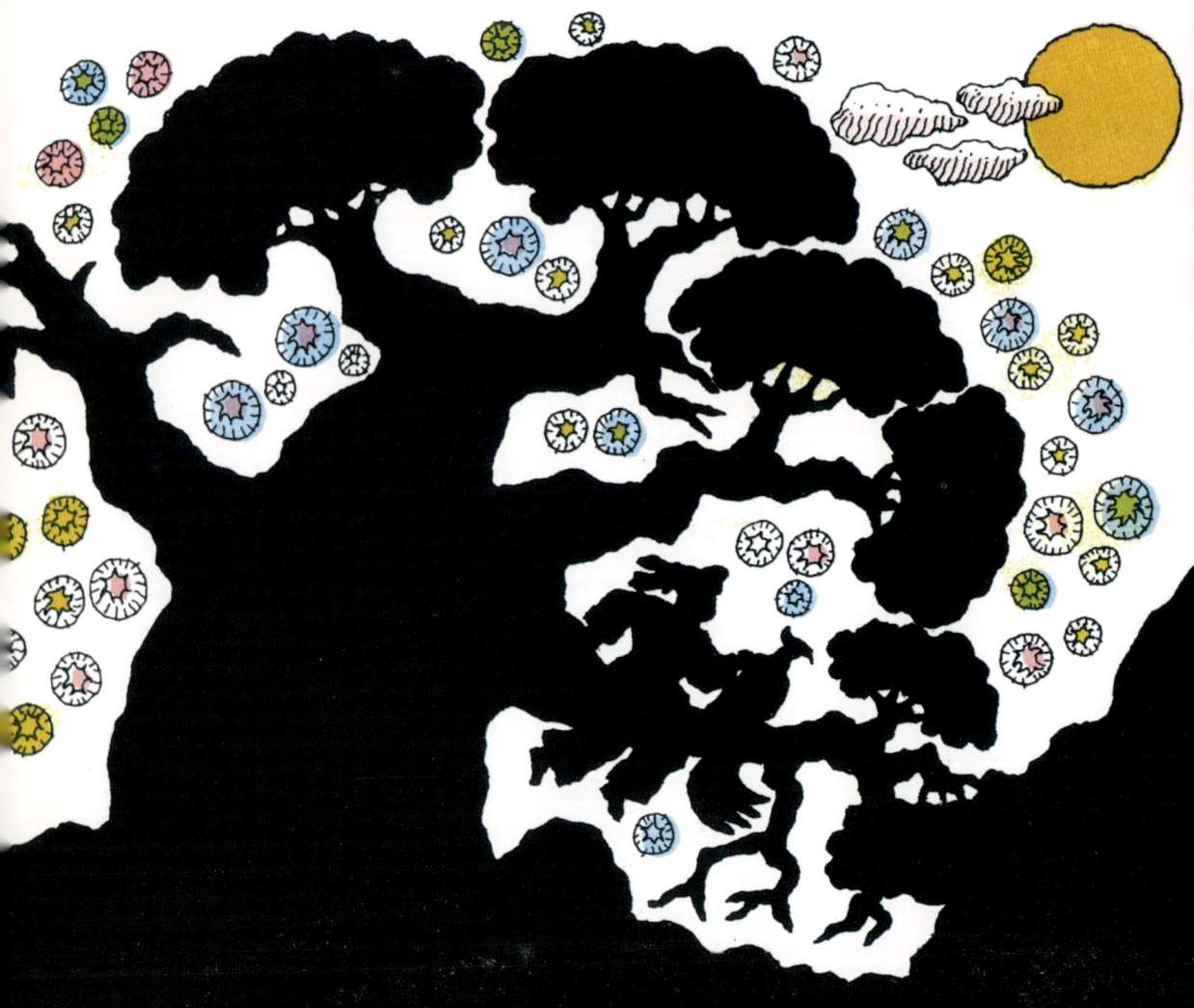

As he climbed down, Don Juan noticed
the big white stones under the Piedras Platas.
And just as the old man had advised him,
he sprinkled holy water on the stones.
And what magic!
The stones turned back into humans!
Don Juan was very glad to see
Don Pedro and Don Diego were among them.

And so the three brothers happily journeyed home.
Don Juan cradled the adarna in his arms.
And just as the king heard the adarna's magical song,
he became strong, healthy and happy again.
The whole kingdom was overjoyed by the good news.
And the moral of the story?
Success is nearest to the one with the kindest heart.